ACT LIKE A LADY
THINK LIKE JESUS

BY

Kathern Ann Thomas

Copyright 2012 by Kathern A. Thomas

All rights reserved

No part of this book may be reproduced, stored in a retrieval system or transmitted by any means without the written permission of the author.

ISBN – 13: 978-1475219234

ISBN – 10: 1475219237

To contact the author:

kathernthomas@aol.com

www.worshippersintercedingforexcellence.com

DEDICATION

This book is dedicated to the memory of

Ethel Saunders,

She was a lady that thought like Jesus.
She was an excellent role model for many
women.

Proverbs 31: 25-31(NIV)

"She is clothed with strength and dignity: She can laugh at the days to come.

She speaks with wisdom, and faithful instruction is on her tongue.

She watches over the affairs of her household and does not eat the bread of idleness.

Her children arise and call her blessed; her husband also, and he praises her:

Many women do noble things, but you surpass them all."

Charm is deceptive, and beauty is fleeting; but a woman who fears the Lord is to be praised. Give her the reward she has earned, and let her works bring her praise at the city gate.

Contents

Chapter 1: Being Divine, Inspirational,
          Victorious &Anointed……………………… 9

Chapter 2: The Samaritan Woman………………….13

Chapter 3: A New Attitude………………………….19

Chapter 4: A Great Demonstration of Love……………..25

Chapter 5: Your Destiny……………………………..31

Chapter 6: Choices…………………………………..33

Chapter 7: A Godly Husband; A Godly Wife………....37

Chapter 8: No Flannel Night Gowns!.......................41

Chapter 9: I'm A Single Lady……………..………….43

Chapter 10: Don't Flirt With Temptation……………....47

Chapter 11: Worry Causes Wrinkles…………….….....55

Chapter 12: Consider Your Ways……………………..61

Chapter 13: Let It Go!......................................63

Chapter 14: When Reality Strikes……………..............71

Chapter 15: Beauty For Ashes………………….….......75

Chapter 16: Leading Ladies of the Bible……………...79

INTRODUCTION

"And now, dear lady, I am not writing you a new command but one we have had from the beginning. I ask that we love one another. And this is love: that we walk in obedience to his commands. As you have heard from the beginning, his command is that you walk in love." 2 John 5 (NIV)

    This book is written to teach Christian women how to behave as ladies using the characteristics of our Lord and Savior, Jesus Christ. Jesus always walked in love. As a Christian woman, God wants you to follow His example. No, I'm not saying you're going to be perfect. God is not asking you to be perfect but He is asking you to be transformed by the renewing of your mind. **Romans 12:2** says, "Do not conform any longer to the pattern of this world, but be transformed by the renewing of your mind. Then you will be able to test and approve what God's will is….his good, pleasing and perfect will."

You might be asking, "How can I renew my mind?" The answer is very simple…….With the Word of God. Of course, you will have to read the Bible. The Bible is our **Basic Instructions Before Leaving Earth!** We need the instructions now. We won't need the instructions in heaven. You can't just read the Bible like it's just another book. You will have to believe that it <u>is</u> the living Word.

When you receive Jesus Christ as your Savior, the Holy Spirit comes to dwell in you and he will help you to understand the Word of God. The carnal mind can only understand what you can hear, see, taste, touch, or feel. We walk by faith, not by sight. By faith, I believe that the Bible was written by men who were inspired by the Holy Spirit. So if Jesus says I can think like Him, I believe it!

1

Being Divine, Inspirational, Victorious & Anointed

Do you know who you are? I want you to know that after you have accepted Jesus Christ, as your Lord and Savior, you are divine, inspirational, victorious, and anointed. You can be a D.I.V.A. for the Kingdom of God *and* a lady

You're not just an ordinary lady. You're a special lady! You are made in the image of our Lord and Savior. You are divine because you were created by God. You are inspirational because you can encourage others with God's Word. You are victorious because Christ died on the Cross to give us victory. You are anointed because the Anointed One lives on the inside of you.

There is something about a real lady. There is an air of confidence, finesse, style, and originality. From the moment a lady steps into the room, everyone knows that she has arrived. Ladies never just walk into a room, they arrive! Their manner sends the signal loud and clear that "I am a lady set apart." They never exit a room without leaving a part of themselves behind. A rich deposit of wisdom, an encouraging word, something seemingly intangible yet profound, that leaves a lasting impression on the hearts of those who interact with them.

A deposit of the divine nature of God was placed into the spirit of every woman when He breathed the breath of life into her and she became a living soul. Every woman is not a lady

But when we examine the attributes of our Savior, we will find that He designed all of us to be ladies.

Divinity and victory are connected. A lady walking in the spirit, knows who she is and whose she is. She has embraced her Savior and yielded to the lordship of Jesus Christ

Thinking Like Jesus

A lady does not compromise her standards because she is sold out to her Lord. Whatever pleases God, pleases her. She knows that if she loves Him, she will obey him.

Thinking Like Jesus

When God sends you a husband, he will not be your "soul mate", he is your "spirit mate".

*

Thinking Like Jesus

You are *divine* because you were created by God. You are *inspirational* because you can encourage others with God's Word. You are *victorious* because Christ died on the Cross to give us victory. You are *anointed* because the Anointed One lives on the inside of you.

2

The Samaritan Woman

In the *Gospel of John, Chapter four,* there was a Samaritan woman, a member of the hated mixed race. She was known to be living in sin, and was in a public place. No respectable Jewish man would talk to a woman under such circumstances. But Jesus did. The gospel is for every person, no matter what his or her race, social position, or past sins.

What did Jesus mean by living water? In Jeremiah 17:13, God is called **"the spring of living water"**. In saying that He would bring living water that could forever quench a person's thirst for God, Jesus was claiming to be the Messiah. Only the Messiah could give this gift that satisfies the soul desire.

As our bodies hunger and thirst so do our souls. But our souls need spiritual food and water. The Samaritan woman confused the two kinds of water because no one else has ever talked to her about her spiritual hunger and thirst before. We don't think of depriving our bodies of food and water when we're hungry or thirsty. Why then should we deprive our souls? The living Word, Jesus Christ, and the written Word, the Bible, can satisfy our hungry and thirsty souls.

Thinking Like Jesus

We must be prepared to share the gospel at any time and in any place. Jesus crossed all barriers to share the gospel, and we must do the same thing.

The woman mistakenly believed that if she received the water Jesus offered, she would not have to return to the well each day. She was interested in Jesus' message because she thought it would make her life easier. Sometimes people accept Christ's message for the wrong reason. Christ did not come to take away challenges. He came to change us on the inside and to empower us to deal with the problems. Paul said, I know Him in the power of the resurrection but now I want to know Him in the fellowship of His sufferings.

Thinking Like Jesus

You don't know Him until you have suffered. The suffering comes with the blessing. Christ said, "If you suffer with me, you will reign with me."

The Samaritan woman did not immediately understand what Jesus was talking about. It takes time to accept something that changes the very foundations of your life. Jesus allowed the woman time to ask questions and put pieces together for herself. You will not always get immediate results when you share the gospel. When you ask people to let Jesus change their lives, give them time to think about it.

When this woman discovered that Jesus knew all about her private life, she quickly changed the subject. Sometimes people become uncomfortable when the conversation is too close to home, and they try to talk about something else. When we witness, we need to just guide the conversation back to Christ and do it in love. The presence of Christ exposes sin and makes people squirm, but only Christ can forgive sins and give new life.

The woman brought up an issue about the correct place to worship. But her question was a smoke screen to keep Jesus away from her deepest need. Jesus directed the conversation to a much more important point: the location of worship is not nearly as important as the attitude of the worshippers. She may have heard about the coming Messiah, but she didn't realize that she was talking to Him!

The "food" that Jesus was talking about was his spiritual nourishment. It includes more than Bible study, prayer, and attending church. Spiritual nourishment also comes from doing God's will and helping to bring his work of salvation to completion.

Thinking Like Jesus

We are nourished not only by what we take *in*, but also what we give *out* for God.

The Samaritan woman was *divine* because she was from God. She was *inspirational* because she left her water jar and went back to the town and said to the people, "Come see a man who told me everything I ever did." She was ***victorious*** because the Bible says, many of the Samaritans from the town believed in Jesus because of her testimony. She was ***anointed*** because the anointing destroyed the yoke of unbelief in the other Samaritans. She was a lady that had a personal encounter with Jesus. Have you had yours?

3

A New Attitude

If you have a bad attitude, you need a new one. If you already have a good attitude, it can still get better. We are supposed to have the mind of Christ and that means we should have the attitude of Christ.

In recently studying about the seven churches in the ***Book of Revelation***, I noticed that the last church, which was the church of Laodicea had a wrong attitude. The word *attitude* means a way of looking at things. They were lukewarm. They were following God halfway. What they could *see* and buy had become more valuable than what is *unseen and eternal*. They failed to see that no matter how much you possess or how much money you make, you have nothing if you don't have a true relationship with Jesus Christ.

In the Book of Genesis, 16th Chapter, Sarai gave Hagar to Abram as a substitute wife. This was a common practice at that time. A married woman who could not have children was shamed by her peers and was often required to give a female servant to her husband in order to produce heirs. The children born to the servant woman were considered the children of the wife. Abram was acting in line with the custom of the day, but his action showed a lack of faith that God would fulfill his promise.

Sarai took matters into her own hands by giving Hagar to Abram. Like Abram, she had trouble believing God's promise. Out of the lack of faith came a series of problems. This is what happens when we take over for God, trying to make his promise come true to efforts that are not in line with his specific directions. When we ask God for something and have to wait, it is a temptation to take matters into our own hands and interfere with God's plans.

Although Sarai arranged for Hagar to have a child by Abram, she later blamed Abram for the results. It's often easier to strike out in frustration and accuse someone else than to admit an error and ask for forgiveness. Adam and Eve did the same thing.

Sarai took out her anger against Abram and herself on Hagar, and her treatment was harsh enough to cause Hagar to run away. Anger, especially when it arises from your own shortcomings, can be dangerous.

Hagar was running away from her mistress and her problem. An angel was sent to her by God to give her this advice: (1) to return and face Sarai, the cause of her problem, and (2) to submit to her. Hagar needed to work on her attitude toward Sarai, no matter how justified it may have been. Running away from our problems does not solve them.

> ### *Thinking Like Jesus*
> It's wise to return to your problems, face them squarely, accept God's promise of help, correct your attitude and act as you should.

In this story, we see three people make serious mistakes because they all had the wrong attitude. (1) Sarai, who took matters into her own hands and gave her maid to Abram. (2) Abram, who went along with the plan but when circumstances began to go wrong, refused to help solve the problem; and (3) Hagar, who ran away from the problem.

In spite of this messy situation, God demonstrated his ability to work in all things for good. Sarai and Abram still received the son they so desperately wanted and God solved Hagar's problem despite Abram's refusal to get involved.

4

A Great Demonstration of Love

There was almost nothing worse than being a widow in the ancient world. Widows were taken advantage of or ignored. They were almost always poverty stricken. According to God's law, the nearest relative of the dead husband should care for the widow; but Naomi had no relatives in Moab, and she did not know if any of her relatives were alive in Israel.

Even in her desperate situation, Naomi had a selfless attitude. Although she had decided to return to Israel, she encouraged Ruth and Orpah to stay in Moab and start their lives over, even though this would mean hardship for her. God wants us to consider the needs of others and not just our own.

The **Book of Ruth** is a perfect example of God's impartiality. Although Ruth belonged to a race often despised by Israel, she was blessed because of her faithfulness. She became a great grandmother of King David and a direct ancestor of Jesus.

Naomi had experienced severe hardships. She had left Israel married and secure; she returned widowed and poor. Naomi changed her name to express the bitterness and pain she felt. Naomi was not rejecting God by openly expressing her pain, however, she seems to have lost sight of the tremendous resources she had in her relationship with Ruth and with God.

When you face bitter times, God welcomes your honest prayers, but be careful not to overlook the love, strength, and resources that He provides in your present relationships. And don't allow bitterness and disappointment to blind you to your opportunities.

Ruth and Naomi's return to Bethlehem was certainly part of God's plan because in this town David would be born and as predicted by the Prophet Micah, Jesus would also be born there. The move that they made was fulfillment of scripture.

Ruth made her home in a foreign land. Instead of depending on Naomi or waiting for good fortune to happen, she took the initiative. She went to work. When Ruth went out to the fields, God provided for her. If you are waiting for God to provide, He may be waiting for you to take the first step to demonstrate just how important your need is.

Ruth's life exhibited admirable qualities: she was hardworking, loving, kind, faithful, and brave. These qualities gained her a good reputation but only because she displayed them consistently in all areas of her life. Wherever Ruth went or whatever she did, her character remained the same.

Thinking Like Jesus

Your reputation is formed by the people who watch you at work, at home, in church. A good reputation comes by consistently living out the qualities you believe in.

Boaz was a man of integrity. He went far beyond the gleaner's law in demonstrating his kindness and generosity. Not only did he allow Ruth to glean in his fields but he also told his workers to let some of the grain fall in her path.

Naomi had felt bitter but her faith in God was still alive, and she praised God for Boaz's kindness to Ruth. We may feel bitter about a situation, but we must never give up.

> ***Thinking Like Jesus***
>
> In her sorrows, she still trusted God and acknowledged his goodness. We have to have faith that God is directing our lives for His purpose.

Ruth may not have realized it but when she went to glean, she didn't just happen to end up in the field with Boaz. God was leading her. God wants you to know today that He is working in your life in ways that you may not even notice.

> ***Thinking Like Jesus***
>
> Whether you're waiting for a husband, a job, a loved one to be saved, or a healing to manifest. You must remember that God knows where you are and as you acknowledge Him in all your ways, He will direct your path.

5

Your Destiny

Acting like a lady, thinking like Jesus will enable you to know your destiny. A lady does not rush into things. In Jeremiah 29:11-13, God says "For I know the plans I have for you, plans to prosper you and not to harm you, plans to give you hope and a future. Then you will call upon me and come and pray to me, and I will listen to you. You will seek me and find me when you seek me with all your heart."

In the ***Book of Genesis,*** Joseph dreamed of his destiny at a very early age. He encountered many trials and tribulations before arriving at his destination. His brothers betrayed him. Potiphar's wife lied on him, his cell mate forgot about him. It was several years before Joseph reached his destination but he held on to his dream and he never gave up.

I never knew that I was called to be a pastor. But when I look back on my life, I can see that God was preparing me for it the whole time. I've always been a very compassionate person, very creative, and very bold. I consider myself to be like Peter. In spite of my poor choices, mistakes, and mischief, God chose to use me to be a shepherd for His sheep. I love pastoring and God uses my natural and spiritual gifts for His glory. I believe I am walking in my destiny.

> ***Thinking Like Jesus***
>
> No problem is too complicated for God if you keep the right attitude and allow Him to help you.

6

Choices

In studying my Bible, I cannot find where Jesus made any wrong choices. When we make the wrong choice, we suffer the consequences. Jesus embodies God in human flesh and blood. If you want to know God's character, look at Jesus and his character.

John 14:20 "On that day you will realize that I am in my Father, and you are in me, and I am in you"

John 1:14 The Word became flesh and made his dwelling among us. We have seen his glory, the glory of the One and Only, who came from the Father, full of grace and truth. Jesus was the embodiment of the fruit of the spirit that is mentioned in Galatians.

Galatians 5:22-23 But the fruit of the Spirit is love, joy, peace, patience, kindness, goodness, faithfulness, gentleness and self-control. Against such things there is no law.

Jesus came to show us what these character traits looked like in human flesh. He was full of kindness, gentleness and goodness and always exercised self-control and longsuffering, even in the most adverse situations. He was full of love, joy and peace as He went about doing His Father's business. When we walk in the Spirit, we will **"Act Like A Lady, Think Like Jesus."** We have to grow into the character of Jesus Christ.

(Ephesians 4:21-24) Surely you heard of Him and were taught in Him in accordance with the truth that is in Jesus. You were taught with regard to your former way of life, to put off your old self, which is being corrupted by its deceitful desires; to be made new in the attitude of your minds; and to put on the new self, created to be like God in true righteousness and holiness.

You're not acting like a lady if you are:

lying to one another

staying angry with one another

stealing from one another

gossiping about one another

not forgiving one another

operating in sexual immorality

These things grieve the Holy Spirit. *Get rid of all bitterness, rage and anger, brawling and slander, along with malice. Be kind and compassionate to one another, forgiving each other, just as in Christ, God forgave you. (Ephesians 4:31-32)*

Remember the choice is up to you! *Be very careful, then how you live….not as unwise but as wise, making the most of every opportunity, because the days are evil. Therefore, do not be foolish, but understand what the Lord's will is. (Ephesians 5:15-17)*

7

A Godly Husband; A Godly Wife

Ephesians 5:25-28 Husbands should love their wives just as Christ loved the church and gave himself up for her to make her holy, cleansing her by the washing with water through the word, and to present her to himself as a radiant church, without stain or wrinkle or any other blemish, but holy and blameless. In the same way, husbands ought to love their wives as their own bodies. He who loves his wife loves himself.

How should a godly husband love his wife?

- He should be willing to sacrifice everything for her.

- He should make her wellbeing of primary importance.

- He should care for her as he cares for his own body.

A wife does not need to fear submitting to a man who treats her in this way.

Ephesians 5:22-23………Wives submit to your husbands as to the Lord. For the husband is the head of the wife as Christ is the head of the church, his body, of which he is the Savior. Now as the church submits to Christ, so also wives submit to their husbands in everything.

Although some people have distorted Paul's teaching on submission by giving unlimited authority to husbands, we cannot get around it……Paul told wives to submit to their husbands.

The fact that a teaching is not popular is no reason to discard it. According to the Bible, the man is the spiritual head of the family, and his wife should acknowledge his leadership. But real spiritual leadership involves service. Just as Christ served the disciples, even to the point of washing their feet, so the husband is to serve his wife.

> ***Thinking Like Jesus***
>
> A wise and Christian husband will not take advantage of his leadership role, and a wise and Christ-honoring wife will not try to undermine her husband's leadership.

The union of husband and wife merges two persons in such a way that little can affect one without also affecting the other. Oneness in marriage does not mean losing your personality in the personality of another. Instead, it means caring for your spouse as you care for yourself, learning to anticipate his or her needs, helping the other person become all he or she can be.

8

No Flannel Night Gowns!

Ladies, when you are single, you can spend all the time you want doing what you think pleases you and God. When you are married, God wants you to spend time pleasing your husband.

It's wrong to make your husband wait for dinner while you are studying the Bible. I was recently told a story about a husband being angry because his wife was locked in the room praying for two hours. The husband was not saved and even if he was, the wife did not make the correct choice. She should have chosen to spend that time with God when her husband was gone or asleep.

Ladies, husbands want your attention! When you are married, your body belongs to your husband. He does not want you to come to bed in a flannel night gown and speaking in tongues. I don't care if you are a pastor of a church, a first lady, or a member. There is a time and a place for everything. I suggest that the two of you agree on the time you will spend together studying the Word and being in prayer.

9

I'm A Single Lady

Yes, I <u>am</u> a single lady and I want to give a few tips to those of you who are single:

- Stop being desperate!
- It's a man's natural instinct to want to take care of a woman.
- Be patient and wait on God.
- The man needs to be in love with God first so he will know how to love his wife.
- No one can love you like Jesus Christ except one of his sons.

6) You need a man who can minister to your mind, body, soul, and spirit.

7) Attract a man with godliness.

8) Keep "Victoria's Secret" a secret. You'll have plenty of time to share "the secret" after marriage.

Ladies, it doesn't matter whether you are single or married because you are no longer behind the veil. In *2nd Corinthians 3:7-11*, Paul contrasts the glory of the Ten Commandments with the glory of the life-giving Spirit. The Spirit gives new life to all who believe in Christ.

Paul is saying that if the old covenant had its glory (and it certainly did), just imagine how glorious the new covenant is. The law was wonderful because, although it condemned us, it pointed us to Christ. But in the new covenant, the law and the promise are fulfilled. Christ has come…..by faith, we are made right with God.

When Moses came down Mount Sinai with the Ten Commandments, his face glowed from being in God's presence. *(Exodus 34:29-35).* Moses had to put on a veil to keep the people from being terrified by the brightness of his face. When anyone becomes a Christian, Jesus removes the veil, giving eternal life and freedom from trying to be saved by keeping laws. Ladies and gentlemen, without the veil, we can be like mirrors reflecting God's glory. *And we, who with unveiled faces all reflect the Lord's glory, are being transformed into his likeness with ever increasing glory, which comes from the Lord, who is the Spirit. (2nd Corinthians 3:18)*

10

Don't Flirt With Temptation

In the *16th Chapter of Judges,* Samson was deceived because he wanted to believe Delilah's lies. Although he could strangle a lion, he could not smother his burning lust and see Delilah for who she really was. How can you keep your desire for love and sexual pleasure from deceiving you? (1) You must decide what kind of a person you will love *before* passion takes over…….. Determine whether a person's character and faith in God are as desirable as his or her physical appearance. (2) Because most of the time you spend with your husband or wife will *not* involve sex, your companion's personality, temperament, and commitment to solve problems must be as gratifying as his or her kisses. (3) Be patient. The second look often reveals what is beneath the pleasant appearance and attentive touch.

Delilah kept asking Samson for the secret of his strength until he finally grew tired of hearing her nagging and gave in. This was the second time that Samson allowed himself to be worn down by persistent nagging. What a pitiful excuse for disobedience. Don't allow anyone, no matter how attractive or persuasive, to talk you into doing wrong.

Delilah was a deceitful woman with honey on her lips and poison in heart. Cold and calculating, she toyed with Samson, pretending to love him while looking for personal gain. How could Samson be so foolish? Four times Delilah took advantage of him. If he did not realize what was happening after the first or second experience, surely he should have understood the situation by the fourth time! We think Samson is foolish, but how many times do we allow ourselves to be deceived by flattery and give in to temptation and wrong beliefs? Ask God to help you distinguish between deception and truth.

Although God did not completely abandon Samson, He allowed Samson's decision to stand, and the consequences of his decision followed naturally. In spite of Samson's past, God still answered his prayer and destroyed the pagan temple and worshippers. God still loved him. He was willing to hear Samson's prayer of confession and repentance and use him this final time. One of the effects of sin in our lives is to keep us from feeling like praying. But perfect moral behavior is not a condition for prayer. Don't let guilty feelings over sin keep you from your only means of restoration. No matter how long you have been away from God, he is ready to hear from you and restore you to a right relationship. Every situation can be salvaged if you are willing to turn again to God. If God could still work in Samson's situation, He can certainly make something worthwhile out of yours.

Samson was a man captive to his own passions and pride. He is not one you would want to emulate. His gifts were great but his flaws were greater. His godly parents had great expectations for his life, but his strong-willed nature drove him to pursue his own pleasures rather than to protect and defend God's people. God gave him great strength to be used for God's people, but instead Samson used his abilities for his own purposes. Samson did not stay close to God, and so he didn't live up to his potential. Although Samson judged Israel for 20 years, he was never the kind of leader the earlier judges were. Samson was a great warrior himself, but he couldn't inspire others to take up the battle. So the Philistines continued to oppress Israel through his 20 years as judge.

There are many lessons to learn from Samson but I want to point out three:

1) **Being gifted does not equate to godliness.** Samson was the most gifted man of his day. He had been given all the tools to do great things for God. Yet in his pride and stubbornness, he lived for his own passions rather than for God's purposes. Today, God has given you the stewardship of both spiritual and physical abilities. Don't waste your potential for serving God and His people. Be a wise steward and put the use of your potential in God's hands, and see how God will multiply it.

2) **God doesn't give up on his children.** Samson made a total mess of his life. He failed to achieve his potential. Yet in the end, he did look to God one last time. God gave him the

strength to strike a severe blow of judgment upon the leadership of the Philistines. Are you feeling guilty and separated from God because of sinful choices? God is ready to hear and forgive and restore you to the joy of fellowship with Him. (Psalm 32)

3) **You must choose to pursue God rather than flirt with temptation**. Samson chose to continue in a compromising relationship with a harlot name Delilah until it cost him his sight, his freedom, and ultimately, his life. Delilah can be a male or a female. The world is your Delilah. My Bible tells me that being a friend to the world is enmity against God.

Don't see how close you can come to temptation by associating with the wrong crowd or by hanging in questionable places or doing questionable things. Instead, see how close you can stay to Jesus. Spend your time learning and growing from relationships with God's people.

Follow the Apostle Paul's advice to his young friend Timothy in 2 Timothy 2:22…. "Flee youthful lusts; but pursue righteousness, faith, love, peace with those who call on the Lord out of a pure heart."

11

Worry Causes Wrinkles

Because of the bad effects of worry, Jesus tells us not to worry about those needs that God promises to supply. Worry can:

- *damage your health*

- *cause the object of your worry to consume your thoughts*
- *disrupt your productivity*

- *cause you to treat others negatively*

- *reduce your ability to trust in God*

The difference between worry and concern is worry immobilizes but concern moves you to action. **"When we have a problem, we need to go to the throne and not the phone!"**

To seek first God's kingdom and his righteousness means to turn to God first for help, to fill your thoughts with his desires, to take his character for your pattern, and to serve and obey him in everything. What is really important to you? People, objects, goals, and other desires all compete for priority in your life. Any of these can quickly bump God out of first place if you don't actively choose to give him first place in <u>every</u> area of your life.

Planning for tomorrow is time well spent but worrying about tomorrow is time wasted. Sometimes it's difficult to tell the difference. Careful planning is thinking about goals, steps, and schedules, and trusting in God's guidance. Planning can help to stop worrying when you do it well. Worriers are consumed by fear and find it difficult to trust God. They let their plans interfere with their relationships with God.

Mary and Martha both loved Jesus. They were both serving him but Martha thought Mary's style of serving was inferior to hers. She didn't realize that in her desire to serve, she was actually neglecting her guest.

Are you so busy doing things for Jesus that you're not spending time with him? "Don't let your service become self-serving."

Eight Reasons Not To Worry....

1) The same God who created life in you can be trusted with the details of your life.

2) Worrying about the future hampers your efforts for today.

3) Worrying is more harmful than helpful.

4) God does not ignore those who depend on him.

5) Worry shows a lack of faith in and understanding of God.

6) There are real challenges that God wants us to pursue, and worrying keeps us from them.

7) Living one day at a times keeps us from being consumed with worry.

8) Worry causes wrinkles!

Remember these scriptures…

1 Peter 5:7

Cast all your care on Him because He cares for you.

Philippians 4:19

And my God will supply all your needs according to his riches in glory through Christ, Jesus.

When Job lost everything that he had, he didn't worry! My Bible tells me that one day the angels came to present themselves before the Lord and Satan came with them. The Lord said to Satan, "Where have you come from?" Satan answered the Lord, "From roaming through the earth and going back and forth in it." Then the Lord said to Satan, "Have you considered my servant Job?" There is no one on earth like him; he is perfect and upright, a man who fears God and shuns evil."

Satan told God, "You have put a hedge of protection around him and his family and everything that he has. But stretch out your hand and strike everything that he has and he will surely curse you to your face. The Lord said to Satan, "Everything he has is in your hands, but on the man himself do not lay a finger." Job lost everything that he had but Job said, "I know my redeemer lives". "He knows the way that I take". "Though he slay me, yet will I trust him". Job didn't worry! Instead of worrying, he prayed for his friends that were speaking against him and the

Bible says, after Job had prayed for his friends, the Lord made him prosperous again and gave him twice as much. I'm sure you can think of some friends who have done you wrong. Don't spend time telling everyone about it. Pray for them. God wants to prosper you.

12

Consider Your Ways

In the **Book of Haggai, Chapter One,** God asked his people how they could live in luxury when his house was lying in ruins. The temple was the focal point of Judah's relationship with God, but it was still demolished. Instead of rebuilding the temple, the people put their energies into beautifying their own home. However, the harder the people worked for themselves, the less they had, because they ignored their spiritual lives. The same happens to us. If we put God first, He will provide for our deepest needs. If we put him in any other place, all our efforts will be futile. Caring only for your own physical needs while ignoring your relationship with God will lead to ruin.

Because the people had not given God first place in their lives, their work was not fruitful or productive, and their material possessions did not satisfy. While they concentrated on building and beautifying their own homes, God's blessing was withheld because they no longer put him in first place. Moses had predicted that this would be the result if the people neglected God.

Judah's problem was confused priorities. Like Judah, our priorities involving occupation, family and God's work are often confused. Jobs, homes, vacations, and leisure activities may rank higher on our list of priorities than God. What is more important to you? Where is God on your list of priorities?

Grain, grapes, and olives were Israel's major crop. The people depended on these for security while neglecting the worship of God. As a result, God sent a drought to destroy their livelihood and called them back to himself.

The people began rebuilding the temple just 23 days after Haggai's first message. Rarely did a prophet's message produce such a quick response. How often we hear a sermon and respond, "That was a good message, Pastor," and then we leave church and don't act on the message. These people put their words into action. When you hear a good sermon or lesson, make plans to put it into practice.

Haggai encouraged the people to finish rebuilding the temple. Opposition from hostile neighbors had caused them to feel discouraged and to neglect the temple, and neglect God. But Haggai's message turned them around and motivated them to pick up their tools and continue the work they had begun.

God wants you to consider your ways!

2nd Corinthians 5:21 says "God made him who had no sins to be sin for us, so that in him we might become the righteousness of God."

If you are the righteousness of God, you should have the fruit of righteousness.

Some of us, no matter what we do, we don't have peace. That's because we're not walking in righteousness and we're always busy but we don't have the confidence that we need to go for the things of God.

God wants us to live in peaceful dwelling places, in secure homes, in undisturbed places of rest. If you do not have peace, consider your ways!

13

Let It Go!

Apostle Paul says that his goal is to know Christ, to be like Christ and to be all Christ has in mind for him. This goal absorbs all Paul's energy. This is a helpful example for us. We should not let anything take our eyes off our goal…..knowing Christ. We must lay aside everything harmful and forsake anything that may distract us from being effective Christians.

We have all done things for which we are ashamed and we are constantly struggling between what we have been and what we want to be. But, because our hope is in Christ, we can let go of past guilt and look forward to what God will help us become. Don't dwell on your past. "Let It Go"! Grow in the knowledge of God by concentrating on your relationship with Him <u>now</u>. Realize that you are forgiven and then move on to a life of obedience and faith. Look forward to a fuller and more meaningful life because of your hope in Christ.

Sometimes trying to live a perfect Christian life can be so difficult that it leaves us drained and discouraged. We may feel so far from perfect that we can never please God with our lives. Paul uses perfect to mean mature or complete, not flawless in every detail.

Three stages of perfection:

Perfect Relationship…..We are perfect because of our eternal union with the infinitely perfect

Christ. When we become his children, we are declared "not guilty," and righteous because of what Christ, God's beloved Son, has done for us. This perfection is absolute and unchangeable, and it is this perfect relationship that guarantees that we will one day be "completely perfect".

Perfect Progress…..We can grow and mature spiritually as we continue to trust Christ, learn more about him, draw closer to him, and obey him. Our progress is changeable because it depends on our daily walk. At times in life we mature more than at other times. But when we PRESS ON, we are growing toward perfection.

Completely Perfect……When Christ returns to take us into his eternal kingdom, we will be glorified and made completely perfect.

All three stages of perfection are grounded in your faith in Christ and what he has done, *not what we can do for him*. We cannot perfect ourselves, only God can work in and through us to carry us on to completion until the day of Christ Jesus.

Those who are mature should press on in the Holy Spirit's power, knowing that Christ will reveal and fill in any discrepancy between what we are and what we should be.

Christian maturity involves acting on the guidance that you have already received. We can always make excuses that we still have so much to learn. God's instruction for you today is to live up to what you already know and live out what you have already learned. Ladies, you can do it!

Paul challenged the Philippians to be more like Christ by following his example. This did not mean that they should copy everything that he did; he had just stated that he was not perfect. But he was saying that as he focused his life on being like Christ, so should they. The fact that God could tell people to follow his example is a testimony to his character. Can you do the same? What kind of follower would a new Christian become if he or she imitated you?

Paul criticized the self-indulgent Christians, people who claim to be Christians but don't live up to Christ's model of servant hood and self-sacrifice. These people satisfied their own desires before even thinking about the needs of others. Freedom in Christ does not mean freedom to be selfish. It means taking every opportunity to serve and to become the best person you can be.

14

When Reality Strikes

In *2nd Chronicles 26th Chapter,* Uzziah lived the first part of his reign fearing God, until he became strong and arrogant. Uzziah overstepped his authority for he thought he was more important than he actually was.

Ladies, many of our disappointments that we experience in our walk with the Lord result from false ideas we have about God's character and nature. These false ideas cause us to expect the Lord to perform in some certain manner, or to maybe overlook some disobedient area of our lives. The Lord teaches us that He will not submit to our concept of Him. When we are confronted with the reality of the situation, we become disappointed. But God does not want us to be surrounded by walls of our own private illusions. He wants us to live in reality. He wants us to know Him for who He is and then we can see ourselves more clearly for what we are.

We often dictate to God what we expect Him to be, but we can only approach the Lord on <u>His terms</u>. King Uzziah learned this lesson in a very painful way. Every time Uzziah saw his own reflection and saw himself covered with leprosy, He was reminded that God is Sovereign.

We too can learn from this episode. We need to pray and ask God to free us from all illusion of our supposed self-importance. God wants to heal us of all false conceptions we have of him and of ourselves.

After God gave Uzziah great prosperity and power, he became proud and corrupt. It's true that pride goes before destruction. God hates pride. It's normal to feel good when we accomplish something, but it's wrong to look down on others. Check your attitude and remember to give God credit for what you have. Use your gifts in ways that please Him.

God expects you to honor, worship, and obey Him. For much of his life, Izaiah did that because the scripture says that Uzziah "did what was right in the eyes of the Lord". But Uzziah turned away from God, and was struck with leprosy and remained leprous until his death. He is remembered more for his arrogant act and subsequent punishment than for his great deeds. God requires lifelong obedience. Spurts of obedience are not enough. Mark 13:13 says, only "he who stands firm to the end" will be rewarded. You want God to remember you for your consistent faith otherwise you too may become more famous for your downfall than for your success.

Uzziah overestimated his own importance because of the great achievements that he had experienced. He did so many things well that a consuming pride gradually invaded his life like the leprous disease that finally destroyed his body. In trying to act like a priest, he took on a role that God did not mean for him to have. He had not only forgotten how much God had given him but also that God had certain roles for others that he needed to respect.

Uzziah's pride was rooted in his lack of thankfulness. The Bible doesn't show us anywhere that he showed appreciation to God for the marvelous gift he received. Lack of thankfulness to God can lead to pride. If you're going to act like a lady and think like Jesus, you will have to walk in humility.

15

Beauty For Ashes

In ***Isaiah, Chapter 61,*** God lets us know that He wants to give us a crown of beauty instead of ashes, the oil of gladness instead of mourning, and a garment of praise instead of a spirit of despair. In my book, **"*Private Hell Public Ministry*",** I have written about being in a marriage for seven years with a verbally abusive husband.

While I was in this marriage, I accumulated many ashes, mourning, and despair. I had a choice to keep those ashes or give them to God. It didn't happen overnight but through a process, God has transformed me into the woman of God that I am today.

When I think about where I might be today, I am constantly praising God for my victory! If I had not forgiven my ex-husband and continued to walk in love, I would not be able to minister to God's people. You can only really minister what's in you.

Maybe, you have gone through an abusive marriage or have been hurt by loved ones close to you. Do yourself a favor and forgive the person. That's being a lady and thinking like Jesus!

"Instead of their shame my people will receive a double portion, and instead of disgrace they will rejoice in their inheritance; and so they will inherit a double portion in their land, and everlasting joy will be theirs." Isaiah 61:7

God loves you so much, He wants you to have his best. Unforgiveness and bitterness will block your blessings. Give God your ashes and receive your crown of beauty today!

All ladies need to wear a crown because we are all queens for the lord.

But I will restore you to health and heal your wounds, declares the Lord……..Jeremiah 31:3

God has restored me to health and healed all my wounds. He wants to do the same for you. I know the devil has told you that you can never trust anyone, but the devil is a liar! If he can keep you believing that, you aren't really trusting God.

I'm not saying that you should trust everyone but a closer walk with God will let you know who you can trust. The Bible teaches us that the Holy Spirit will lead and guide us into all truth.

Now that I have my "crown of beauty", no one is going to make me take those ashes back!

Leading Ladies of the Bible
Synopses

Eve	*Page 81*
Sarah	*Page 83*
Miriam	*Page 85*
Zipporah	*Page 87*
Deborah	*Page 89*
Ruth	*Page 91*
Hannah	*Page 93*
Abigail	*Page 95*
The Queen of Sheba	*Page 97*
Huldah	*Page 99*
Esther	*Page 101*
Elisabeth	*Page 103*
Mary Magdalene	*Page 105*
Dorcas	*Page 107*

EVE

The story of the first woman begins with Eve in the Garden of Eden, where she first discovered that she bore a unique relationship to God, the supreme power in the universe. The great reality is not that she came from the rib of Adam but that God created her and brought her womanly nature into being.

The magnificent theme of the story is that God, seeing the incompleteness of man standing alone, wanted to find a helper for him. Not having found this helper in all created things, such as the birds of the air or the beasts of the field, God made a helper for man who was His equal and who shared in the same processes of creation in which He shared. God created this helper, Eve whose name means "life", not from the animal kingdom, but from the rib of Adam himself.

Eve herself, like all of us, came into a universe that was immeasurable an orderly, and her creation takes on the same Wonder as that of the stars, the sun, the moon, and all other things which God created and called good.

When Eve listened to the serpent, representing temptation, she followed, not the will of God, but the path of evil. When she ate the fruit from the Forbidden Tree, she acted independently of God, in whose image she had been created.

After she had partaken of the forbidden fruit, she also gave it to Adam, and he too ate it, thus sharing in her guilt. In this act, we have an excellent example of woman's impulsiveness and man's inclination to follow a woman wherever she leads, unfortunately, even into sin.

SARAH

The first woman distinctly portrayed in the dramatic history of man's spiritual development is Sarah, beloved wife of Abraham, founder of the House of Israel.

Sarah's life was one continuous trial of her faith in God's promise that she was to be the Mother of Nations. Through this trial, she emerged as a woman of power, one who was a dutiful and beloved wife.

In Sarah's period, which was probably sometime in the nineteenth or twentieth century B.C., a woman assumed little importance until she had given her husband a son, for it was through his son that a man lived on. The tragedy of Sarah's early life was that she was barren, but the miracle of her life was that she gave birth to Isaac, Son of Promise, when, humanly speaking, the time had passed when she could become a mother.

The miracle was achieved through the faith of Abraham and the loyalty of Sarah to her husband. While they still resided at Haran, God said to Abraham, "Get thee out of thy country, and from thy kindred, and from thy father's house, unto a land that I will show you; and I will make of thee a great nation."

Sarah was the first woman to go through reverse menopause. God, not only renewed her womb but at the age of 90, she was still so beautiful that the king desired to steal her from Abraham.

Sarah's life became Abraham's. Where he went she went, not as his shadow but as a strong influence. Her love and loyalty were blessed by Abraham's devotion to her.

MIRIAM

We have the first picture of her in *Exodus 2:4-7,* when she was a little girl. Here she is not named, but referred to only as Moses' sister. Her courage at this time gives an indication of the kind of woman she was to become.

As she stood guarding her baby brother in the ark made by their mother Jochebed, she exhibited a fearlessness and self-possession unusual in a little girl. She was then probably about seven years old. Though she was awaiting the coming of a powerful princess, the daughter of a hostile tyrant who had decreed that all male babies should be destroyed, Miriam showed poise, intelligence, and finesse. When the daughter of Pharaoh came down with her maidens to the banks of the Nile to bathe and found the little Moses lying there in his ark, Miriam approached her quietly, asking if she would like her to find a Hebrew woman to nurse the baby. Never disclosing by look or word her own relationship to the child, she brought her mother Jochebed to Pharaoh's daughter. The child Moses was safe at last behind palace walls, with his own mother as his nurse.

Miriam is the first woman singer on record. She sang to the Lord using her great gift for the elevation of her people. With her they exulted over their escape from their enemies and with freedom came a newly discovered faith and confidence in God. This was Miriam's greatest hour. She was the new Israel's most renowned woman, and her people held her in high regard.

ZIPPORAH

Zipporah was one of seven daughters and met Moses in the land of Midian soon after he fled there because he had slain an Egyptian, who was beating a Hebrew, one of his own brethren.

Zipporah and her sisters, who had been tending their father's sheep had come with their flocks to draw water at the well. Moses gave water to the sister's sheep. They went home and told their father, who offered Moses the hospitality of his house. Zipporah's marriage to Moses after that is recorded briefly in ***Exodus 2:21.***

Zipporah had two sons and only one was circumcised. When Moses started back from Midian to the Land of Egypt, his wife and his sons were with him. When they stopped at an inn for the night, Moses became very ill. He became so ill that his life was in danger.

When Zipporah saw her husband so violently ill, she believed God was angered with him because he had not circumcised his son. She then seized a piece of flint and circumcised her son herself. She saved her husband's life.

Ladies, sometimes God will use you to save your husband's spiritual life. We should not be quick to give up on our husbands when they are going through a difficult time. Trust God and listen to the Holy Spirit.

DEBORAH

The only woman in the Bible who was placed at the height of political power by the common consent of the people was Deborah. Though she lived in the time of the "Judges," some thirteen centuries before Christ, there are few women in history who have attained the public dignity and supreme authority of Deborah.

In all of her roles, first that of counselor to her people, next as a judge in their disputes, and finally as deliverer in time of war, Deborah exhibited womanly excellence. She was indeed "a mother in Israel." She arose to great leadership because she trusted God implicitly and because she could inspire in others that same trust.

She had the courage to summon one of Israel's most capable military men, Barak, from his home in Kedesh. Together they worked out a plan for action against the enemy. Deborah let Barak know she was not afraid of Sisera, commander of Jabin's army; neither was she afraid of his 900 chariots. She made him feel that the spirit that could animate an army was greater than either weapons or fortifications. Probably, she recalled to him that God had led the Israelites through the Sea of Reeds and had broken a mighty oppressor, Pharaoh. And she made Barak realize that God, who had proved himself to be mightier than Pharaoh, also was mightier than Barak's enemies.

Her glorious victory is best recorded in these concluding but meaningful lines of her Bible biography: *"And the land had rest for forty years"* ***(Judges 5:31).***

RUTH

Ruth, the central figure in the Book of Ruth, is one of the most lovable women in the Bible. Her abiding love embraces the person you would least expect it to, her mother-in-law, Naomi.

Naomi was a Hebrew from Bethlehem, while Ruth was a foreigner from Moab, a lofty tableland to the east of the Dead Sea. Though of a neighboring people, hated by early Israel, Ruth finally won her way into their hearts as the ideal daughter-in-law, wife, and mother. The people of the little town of Bethlehem admired her, not because of her genius or her foresight or her great beauty, but because of her womanly sweetness. Her story which finally culminates in her marriage to Boaz, a man of influence, is one of the most beautiful romances in the Bible.

Love worked a miracle in Ruth's life. She was beloved by all because she was so lovable. She proved that love can lift one out of poverty and obscurity, love can bring forth a wonderful child, love can shed its rays, like sunlight, on all whom it touches, even a forlorn and weary mother-in-law. Ruth's love even penetrated the barriers of race.

Old and weary, Naomi longed to return to the land of her birth. All three women wept as they stood to say good-by. Naomi pleaded with her two daughters-in-law to turn back to their mother's house. Orpah did turn back, but Ruth clung lovingly to her mother-in-law, and as she did she made this most wonderful confession of love ever spoken by a daughter-in-law, *"Don't urge me to leave you or to turn back from you. Where you go I will go, and where you stay I will stay. Your people will be my people and your God my God. Where you die I will die, and there I will be buried."*

HANNAH

The woman who personifies the ideal in motherhood in the Old Testament is Hannah, a mother of Samuel, the earliest of the great Hebrew prophets after Moses. Hannah's story, told in the first two chapters of the first Bible book bearing her son's name, breathes of her love and care of her firstborn, the worthy son of a worthy mother.

Hannah's environment was not conducive to prayer, because the people of Israel had lapsed from the high stands of morality and spirituality set up by Moses. She had to break away from old traditions and find a new path. Her husband, Elkanah was a good but easygoing, undistinguished priest; and his other wife, Peninnah, had children, while Hannah had gone.

But Hannah believed with all her heart that God was the creator of children and that only God could convert a woman into a mother. Every year she went from her home at Ramah to the temple at Shiloh, and her most ardent prayer was for a child. This continued reverence was significant. It showed she was not one to pray once and be satisfied, but was willing to pray again and again. When her prayer was answered and there was born to her a son, she named him Samuel, meaning "asked of the Lord". In her loving care of Samuel, Hannah becomes the prototype of the good mother everywhere, setting a stirring example of high morality and spirituality, which could bring a new order into the world.

ABIGAIL

We have the Biblical record that Abigail was of a beautiful countenance as well as a woman of good understanding. But in the next phrase her first husband, Nabal, is described as "churlish and evil in his doings". His most foolish act was directed at David, who had sent ten of his men up to the hills to ask for a little food during feasting time.

David and his men had helped Nabal's shepherds to protect their master's large herds of sheep and goats. Nabal refused to give the men food and David was angry. Being a wise woman, Abigail lost no time, for she knew what happened when strong-minded men like David were angered. She also knew how rashly her husband acted when he was drunk.

She hastily prepared special foods for David's six hundred men. She had everything loaded on donkeys and mounted a donkey herself. In all humility, she approached David and began to intercede for her husband. She begged David to receive the food. She praised David telling him that evil would not be found in him so long as he lived.

When Abigail arrived home, she found her husband still feasting and drinking. She did not tell him of her journey until morning. When the sober Nabal learned from Abigail how near he had come to being slain by David and his men and what she had done to avoid such an attack, he became violently ill. Ten days later he died.

David, later learned of Nabal's death and affectionately remembered the woman of good understanding, who had come over the mountain on a donkey bringing food. He sent his servants to bring her to him and made her his wife. God will always rescue his ladies.

THE QUEEN OF SHEBA

The first reigning queen on record who competed her wits and wealth against those of a king was the Queen of Sheba. She came to Jerusalem from her kingdom of Saba in southwestern Arabia to investigate all that she had heard about Solomon, Israel's wisest and wealthiest king.

She was one of the many rulers from far and wide who sought to learn about Solomon's wisdom. Others sent ambassadors, but she was the only one to go herself. She was a courageous, resourceful woman, who took an active part in increasing the prosperity of her own people. In this, she was successful.

King Solomon's wisdom and the magnificence of his palace and other public buildings surpassed her expectations. After viewing all his splendor and receiving lavish gifts herself, she made the famous comment, "I believed not the words, until I came and mine eyes had seen it: and behold, the half was not told me."

Her visit was so well known to the people of Israel that the story of it was handed down even to Jesus' time, and his reference to her is recorded in *Matthew 12:42 and Luke 11:31.*

The Queen of Sheba, who came to prove, lives on now, nearly thirty centuries since her visit, as a woman whose spirit of adventure and whose resourcefulness, courage, and curiosity have not been surpassed by any queen in history. Her sense of good public and international relations is unparalleled among women of the Bible.

HULDAH

Though many of the Hebrews were given to idolatry and were ignorant of God, still the lamp of divine truth was kept burning in the heart of a woman. That woman was Huldah.

To a high degree, Huldah possesses two great qualities, righteousness and prophetic insight, and because she possessed the former she was able to use the latter wisely. This prophetic power, never trusted to the undeserving, was given to her because she loved God with all her heart.

Evidently Huldah was known in the kingdom of Judah far and wide or she would never have been sought out by King Josiah, who sent five of his own personal messengers to her with the Book of the Law, which had been recently discovered during repairs in the Temple at Jerusalem. He had faith in Huldah's spiritual powers and he wanted her to tell him whether the book was genuine or not.

Huldah's prophecy gave King Josiah greater courage to put into action the laws written in the Book of the Law, which had been sent to her for verification. After this, Josiah had the scroll read in the house of the Lord and made a covenant to walk after the Lord and keep His commandments. Because of this, he fought evil in Judah more zealously.

Only a woman who studied immutable spiritual laws and who prayed unceasingly could have been given insight into the mystery of the future.

ESTHER

Esther is the central figure in what is one of the most controversial books in the Old Testament, because not once does God appear in it. But it's significant and importance to Jewish history stem from the fact that it has become a patriotic symbol to a persecuted people of the ultimate triumph of truth and justice. The courage of Esther became the dominating factor in the salvation of her people.

Like many great characters in history, Esther makes her first appearance as one of the humblest of figures, an orphan Jewess. But four years later, she rises to the position of a queen of amazing power, a power which she manages to use wisely.

The queen who preceded Esther was Vashti, respected as a woman of nobility and honor and one who had the courage to refuse an unjust command from her husband.

Vashti's refusal opened the way for the coming of Esther, who had been reared by her cousin Mordecai, a Benjamite official at the palace gate. He had seen the king's royal notice that beautiful young virgins would be assembled for the king's harem in Shushan, and that the maiden who pleased the king would take the place of Vashti. So Mordecai sent forth his lovely cousin Esther.

Queen Esther soon gained favor with the people when she showed that she had sound judgment, self-control, and the ability to think of others first. It was not long before she learned that Haman, her husband's favorite, hated her people and demanded that they bow down to him. Opposed to such powers of evil as Haman possessed, Esther defended her people with her own life.

A lady thinking like Jesus always puts others before herself.

ELISABETH

Elisabeth holds two distinctions that lend immortality to her name. She was the mother of John the Baptist, forerunner of the Messiah, and she was the first to greet her cousin Mary as mother of the Messiah.

Like her husband, Zacharias, Elisabeth was a godly person. She was not only the wife of a priest but the daughter of a family of priests of the house of Aaron.

As the wife of a priest, Elisabeth gave loving attention to other husband's priestly vestments and to her home, where godly people came to talk over Temple matters. We have Biblical record that both Elisabeth and her husband were *"righteous before God, walking in all the commandments and ordinances of the Lord blameless"* **(Luke 1:6).**

Elisabeth is introduced by Luke as a woman well stricken in years and barren, just as had been

Isaac's, Sarah. To Elisabeth if was foretold that her son would "be great in the sight of the Lord,......*and he shall be filled with the Holy Ghost, even from his mother's womb"*
(Luke 1:15).

In the sixth month that Elisabeth was with child, her cousin Mary, the Virgin, now in Nazareth, received word that she would have a son and that his name would be called Jesus. Mary had greater faith when the angel explained to her, *"And behold, your cousin Elisabeth, she has also conceived a son in her old age: and this is the sixth month with her, who was called barren"* **(Luke 1:36).** The women now had a common bond. They knew that with God nothing was impossible.

MARY MAGDALENE

Christ's empty tomb was first seen by Mary Magdalene, and she was the first to report to the disciples the miracle of the Resurrection, the greatest event the Christian world has ever known.

One of the most stirring narratives in literature is John's description of Mary Magdalene's visit to the tomb. He depicts her as being alone. Other gospel writers say that other women were with her.

Evidently, going on ahead, Mary Magdalene saw that the big circular stone had been rolled back along the groove and had left the entrance clear. Hastening to Peter and "the other disciple, whom Jesus loved" who is thought to be John, she told them, "They have taken away the Lord out of the tomb, and we know not where they have laid him".

These disciples followed Mary Magdalene to the tomb. John went in first and gazed in silent wonder at the open grave, and then Peter came and saw that the grave was empty and that the linen cloths were laying neatly folded in the empty tomb.

From the Scriptures, it is easy to conclude that she was one of the influential women of the town of Magdala, who gave of her substance as well as herself to Jesus' ministry. She had profound gratitude in her heart for his healing of the seven demons with which she had been afflicted.

Jesus had healed her and she had become His faithful and devoted follower. And after his healing, she became a fully poised women, one who could watch at the tomb quietly and unafraid.

DORCAS

Benevolent, compassionate, and devout woman that she was, Dorcas gave so generously of herself to others that her name today, 2,000 years later, is synonymous with acts of charity.

With her sewing needle as her tool and her home as her workshop, she established a service that has reached to the far corners of the earth. We can infer that Dorcas was a woman of affluence. She could have given of her coins only, but she chose to give of herself also.

Though the Bible does not record exact details, we can be sure that Dorcas, with her nimble fingers, stitched layettes for babies, made cloaks, robes, sandals, and other wearing apparel for poverty-stricken widows, the sick and the aged. Many of those in need were downcast because they had to wear rags, but once clothed in the well-fitted garments she made for them, they went away renewed in spirit. No doubt, the people she helped pondered on what would happen to them if she should die. One day, as the people had feared, Dorcas was seized with illness. Death came suddenly.

The disciples sent two men to Peter to ask if he would come to them without delay. Dismissing the weepers, Peter knelt down and prayed over Dorcas. He laid his hands on the head of the woman. In a positive tone of voice, he said to her, "Tabitha, arise".

The Bible says, "And she opened her eyes: and when she saw Peter, she sat up". Then he called the saints and widows and presented Dorcas back to them.

Prayer of Salvation

Father God, I believe in my heart that Jesus is your only begotten son. I believe He died on the cross for my sin. I believe that He rose from the dead and ascended into heaven. I turn away from sin and turn to Jesus. Thank you for forgiving me. I accept Jesus as my Savior and my Lord. In Jesus' Name

Amen

Receive your

"spiritual makeover"

at

www.calledtobeadiva.com

Other Books by Kathern A. Thomas

Celebrating Celibacy

Celebrating Celibacy Devotional Journal

Private Hell Public Ministry

The Struggle Is Over! No More Religion

Books may be purchased on the website:

www.worshippersintercedingforexcellence.com

or www.amazon.com

Made in the USA
Columbia, SC
23 April 2023